398.2454 Peebles
Demons and dragons

11/10/2015

P9-CCO-826

Mythical Beasts

DEMONS AND DRAGONS

Thanks to the creative team:
Senior Editor: Matthew Rake
Designer: Lauren Woods and collaborate agency

Original edition copyright 2015 by Hungry Tomato Ltd.

Copyright © 2016 by Lerner Publishing Group, Inc.

Hungry Tomato™ is a trademark of Lerner Publishing
Group, Inc.

All rights reserved. International copyright secured.
No part of this book may be reproduced, stored in a
retrieval system, or transmitted in any form or by any
means electronic, mechanical, photocopying, recording, or
otherwise without the prior written permission of Lerner
Publishing Group, Inc., except for the inclusion of brief
quotations in an acknowledged review.

Hungry Tomato™
A division of Lerner Publishing Group, Inc.
241 First Avenue North
Minneapolis, MN 55401 USA

For reading levels and more information, look up this title
at www.lernerbooks.com.

Main body text set in Galahad Std 12/1.5
Typeface provided by Adobe Systems.

Library of Congress Cataloging-in-Publication Data

Peebles, Alice, author.
    Demons & dragons / by Alice Peebles ; illustrated by Nigel Chilvers.
       pages cm. — (Mythical beasts)
    "Original Edition Copyright © 2016 Hungry Tomato Ltd."
    Audience: Ages 8-12
    Audience: Grades 4 to 6
    Includes bibliographical references and index.
    ISBN 978-1-4677-6341-7 (lb : alk. paper) — ISBN 978-1-4677-7651-6
(pb : alk. paper) — ISBN 978-1-4677-7215-0 (eb pdf)
    1. Animals, Mythical—Juvenile literature. 2. Monsters—Juvenile
literature. 3. Mythology—Juvenile literature. I. Chilvers, Nigel, illustrator.
II. Title. III. Title: Demons and dragons.
GR825.P38 2016
398.24'54—dc23   2015002071

Manufactured in the United States of America
1 – VP – 7/15/15

Mythical Beasts

DEMONS AND DRAGONS

By Alice Peebles

Illustrated by Nigel Chilvers

HUNGRY TOMATO™

Minneapolis

"On a bleak, lonely heath by a river, Fafnir guarded his pile of treasure . . . and guarded it well. Human skulls and bones scattered all around were proof of that."

Contents

Demons and Dragons

Meet the ten nastiest, weirdest, and scaliest creatures that have ever leaped out of the ocean or winged down from the sky to terrorize tiny people . . .

For as long as humans have existed, they've told tales of demons and dragons that have haunted the world. Demons, or evil spirits, appear in myths from cultures around the globe. They might sound familiar, but have you heard of the Oni of Japan? This huge, horned ogre-like being feeds on human flesh and can even swallow a person whole. What about the shape-shifting Leyak of Bali in Indonesia? These disembodied heads hover around graveyards at night, and some say they feed on blood. Other top tormentors are the Furies of Greek mythology, who harass wrongdoers both during and after life.

Dragons are among the most dangerous mythical creatures. They have tough, scaled serpent bodies, often with legs to stride the earth or wings to fly over it. Many of them breathe fire, and some hoard gold and other treasures in their lairs.

You wouldn't want to run into the Germanic lindwurm or the seven-headed dragon. These beasts come up from the depths of their watery homes to grab meals (human or animal), so the surrounding shore or countryside become no-go areas. But which of these is the most ferocious of all? You're about to find out.

Each of the ten beasts is shown in a vivid scene that catapults you straight into the middle of the action . . . so you'll see each monster's grotesque attributes as it ambushes its prey. The monsters appear in ranked order of power, with scores from 1 to 10 for each of five categories: Strength, Repulsiveness, Special Powers, Ferocity, and Invincibility. You'll also find a suggestion on how to defeat or neutralize each one . . . which shouldn't stop you imagining your own methods!

You can read about the sources of each beast's myth, then turn to the back to find out more. Step up to meet the frightful Echidna, whose human upper half turns into a coiled serpent, and that other horrific hybrid, the Chimera of the three heads, scorching breath, and serpent's tail. Take them on before they take you on!

Menace in the Swamp
The Lindwurm

For once the sun had pierced the fog covering the bottom of the steep valley. Aha, a cool drink on a warm day! The young bullock was sturdy and strong, but he suddenly seemed no more than a toy as a towering serpent parted the waters and leapt toward him. Bucking and bellowing, the bullock struggled against the lindwurm's fangs, but his efforts only hurt him more. With a hollow, rumbling gurgle, both monster and prey sank down to the depths below.

How to defeat a lindwurm

One story tells how some knights tempted a lindwurm into the open with a well-fed, chained bull. Then, as the lindwurm was tussling with its meal, the knights surrounded it and beat it with spiked clubs.

Beast Power

Strength
7

Repulsiveness
2

Special Powers
1

Ferocity
7

Invincibility
6

Total
23/50

Where does this myth come from?

The lindwurm in various guises has entwined itself around all the mythologies of northern Europe, from Germany to Norway. According to legend behind this particular story, the city of Klagenfurt in Austria was founded on the spot where a lindwurm was slain. The city's emblem is a winged serpent or dragon set against a tower.

Floating Heads
Leyak

The moon cast a sickly light over the graveyard as eerie shapes drifted here and there on sinister business. One pulled a newly buried corpse from the ground and dug its sharp fangs into the body. A weird inner glow showed what exactly these creatures were: disembodied heads propelled by the pulsating movement of their own entrails, like the tentacles of a jellyfish.

How to defeat a Leyak

In the daytime, a Leyak has a normal human form, but this person is really a sorcerer, learning or practicing magic. A Leyak can be vanquished in its transformed shape by severing the head from its entrails, or by hiding the body it has become detached from.

Where does this myth come from?

These demons are part of local lore on the island of Bali in Indonesia. They are believed to damage crops, live on blood, and harm people. Islanders avoid graveyards at night and leave gifts outside their homes to appease them. Some villages have elaborate gates, and houses have concealed entrances to keep out the bad magic.

Beast Power

Strength
3

Repulsiveness
9

Special Powers
7

Ferocity
2

Invincibility
3

Total
24/50

Hoarder of Treasure
Fafnir

His scales were fiery red and hard as steel. His head bristled with horns, spikes, and fangs. And he had one passion: gold! Fafnir guarded his pile of treasure well. Human skulls and bones scattered all around were proof of that. Fafnir lifted his great bulk upright with the litheness of a cat and snorted out scalding steam. He sensed an alien presence. Did a mortal dare to challenge him for his treasure?

How to defeat Fafnir

The warrior Sigurd finally killed this fire-breather. He hid in a pit that he had dug between the dragon's cave and the river. When the dragon came down to drink, Sigurd pierced Fafnir's soft underbelly with the god Odin's sword, Gram.

8

Beast Power

Strength
7

Repulsiveness
3

Special Powers
2

Ferocity
7

Invincibility
6

Total
25/50

Where does this myth come from?

The tale is part of Norse mythology, told in the Icelandic Völsunga Saga *or Saga of the Volsungs, written in the late thirteenth century. Volsung was a mighty warrior and king of the Huns, and the brave hero Sigurd was his grandson. The stories involve battle and betrayal, vengeance and friendship, and Sigurd is a key player.*

Earth Scorcher
The Firedrake

A shepherd was driving his flock out to pasture. He looked up in surprise as a chill wind stirred the air and the sky darkened. A sinister shape was blocking out the sun. In seconds, it was overhead: a snapping firedrake, blackening the grass with its breath.

In panic, the sheep stampeded away, but not before the creature had swooped upon two of them with an exultant roar. Sparks rained down as the monster wheeled in the air and headed back to its lair, clutching the plump bodies.

How to defeat a firedrake

A Polish firedrake called the Wawel Dragon was outwitted by a cobbler, who left a dead lamb packed with sulfur outside the dragon's cave. After eating it, the dragon drank so much water that it swelled up like a balloon and exploded.

Where does this myth come from?

Firedrake stories are common in northern European mythology of the Middle Ages. The Wawel Dragon was named after Wawel Hill, near Krakow in Poland, where it lived in a cave. The earliest account of the creature dates from the twelfth century. There is even a statue of the dragon outside Wawel Cathedral.

Beast Power

Strength 7

Repulsiveness 4

Special Powers 3

Ferocity 6

Invincibility 7

Total 27/50

Terror at the Gates
The Oni

A cloud of fear hung over the village. For months, an Oni had been lurking by the village gates at dusk and snatching stray passersby. It lived on blood and bone marrow, so people said. At last a brave samurai called Aki declared, "Enough! Shame on us for our fear!"

That evening Aki and his comrades crept down to the gate and waited in the shadows. At last, a gruesome shape swept into view. It was ten times as tall as the samurai, with horns and large fangs. With his sword, Aki sliced through a vein in the creature's arm. The Oni howled in fury and lashed out. Battle had commenced . . .

How to defeat an Oni

In traditional exorcism rites, people threw peaches at a representation of the demon to chase an Oni away. The fruit was believed to have power over malicious spirits. People might also throw beans and even sardine heads to ward off the Oni.

Where does this myth come from?

Oni are famous in Japanese mythology. The most fearsome bring disaster and death to the world and feed on human flesh. These are the spirits of the dead who carry resentment and hatred into the afterlife. A collection of one thousand tales from the Heian period (794–1185 CE) feature male and female Oni, both equally feared.

Beast
Power

Strength
8

Repulsiveness
7

Special Powers
2

Ferocity
7

Invincibility
6

Total
30/50

The Beast from the Sea
The Seven-Headed Dragon

The maiden shut her eyes, shivering with cold and fear on the lonely rock. A swirling wind seemed to be blowing some mysterious crested islands toward the shore. Then the islands rose out of the sea! A monster with seven dragons' heads was pounding through the shallows toward her. She could see spines ranged along its seven muscular necks, while its leathery wings created a whirlwind of sea spray. Then one of the heads lashed out as fast as a cobra's to snatch the small, crumpled human.

———◆•◆•◆———

How to defeat a seven-headed dragon

Perhaps a huge pit could be dug on the seashore, lined with stakes and concealed under seaweed. As the dragon lunges for its prey, it could fall in and be impaled.

Beast Power

Strength
8

Repulsiveness
8

Special Powers
3

Ferocity
8

Invincibility
7

Total
34/50

Where does this myth come from?

The seven-headed dragon occurs in legends from regions and places as far apart as Cambodia, India, Persia, and East Africa. In a Japanese version of the story, the dragon comes ashore to claim its yearly meal of a young girl. The hero saves her by stupefying the dragon with a tempting potion, then slaying it.

Mother of all Monsters
Echidna

A scourge to humankind and a pest to the gods, foul Echidna lay curled up in her cave. A deluge of rain had swept the earth, sending a torrent of water pouring through a crevice. She raised her head and peered around the gloom. What had landed on her tail? It squirmed and shouted. And so did something else.

Not one but two humans had landed in her coils, swept down from above. One, half-choking on her poisonous stench, struggled to clamber over her slimy python's body, even as she entwined his companion in her tail . . .

------◆•◆------

How to defeat Echidna

The immortal Echidna was seemingly invincible. But some myths say that the all-seeing giant Argus killed her while she slept in her cave. Perhaps he took her by surprise and used his superhuman strength, or perhaps he was helped by the goddess Hera, whom he served.

Where does this myth come from?

Echidna, whose name means "female viper," is one of the main monsters of Greek mythology. In his poem Theogony, *about the family tree of the gods, Hesiod describes her snake-like ability to strike quickly. Her preferred diet, of course, was human flesh.*

4

Beast Power

Strength
9

Repulsiveness
9

Special Powers
1

Ferocity
10

Invincibility
9

Total
38/50

Fire-Breathing Fiend
The Chimera

Black smoke and molten lava filled the air as the cattle bolted in terror. In pursuit came an unearthly creature, part dragon, part lion, part goat. Its dragon's mouth breathed fire, while the other heads roared with bloodthirsty excitement. The huge, powerful body pounced on one of the mighty cows, pinning it to the ground as easily as a cat trapping a mouse under its paw. The Chimera delivered a crushing bite and her prey fell silent.

How to defeat the Chimera

The Greek hero Bellerophon was given the perilous task of slaying the Chimera. Riding the winged horse, Pegasus, he thrust a lead-tipped lance into her fire-breathing mouth, so that she suffocated as the lead melted.

Beast Power

Strength
9

Repulsiveness
9

Special Powers
3

Ferocity
9

Invincibility
9

Total
39/50

Where does this myth come from?

The Chimera was a monster of Greek mythology that devastated ancient Lycia in present-day Turkey. Homer mentions her in his epic poem about the Trojan War, The Iliad. Around 77 CE the Roman writer Pliny the Elder connected her with constant volcanic activity on Mount Chimaera in Lycia. The rocks there are still dotted with fires fuelled by the methane gas below.

2

All-Powerful Serpent
Illuyanka

As the ocean darkened and broke into an infinity of waves, Teshub the storm god swept down from the heavens. He called out in thunderous tones, "I see you, Illuyanka! You wish to challenge my power over sky and land! Come forth and do battle!"

The snake's head reared up from the water. His coils looped back toward the horizon. Now he gathered them together like a giant spring and delivered a crippling sideways blow to the god. Then he ripped out one of Teshub's eyes. As blood poured from the socket, Illuyanka reached for his other eye. The heart would be next . . .

How to defeat Illuyanka

Teshub had his revenge through his son, Sarruma, who married the daughter of Illuyanka. Thanks to her, Sarruma could reclaim his father's eyes and heart. Once restored, Teshub at last killed the serpent. Without such powerful kin, it would be difficult to overcome the giant sea snake.

Where does this myth come from?

The story belongs to Hittite mythology. The Hittites were an ancient people. Starting around 1600 BCE they lived in the land that eventually became Turkey. The legend of Illuyanka was carved and illustrated on clay tablets. It is written in the ancient wedge-shaped script called cuneiform.

Beast Power

Strength
10

Repulsiveness
9

Special Powers
3

Ferocity
9

Invincibility
9

Total
40/50

Underworld Tormentors
The Furies

"Mercy! Mercy!" in despair, the man fell to his knees. A pitiless screeching heralded the arrival of the Furies, sent by the god of darkness to deliver eternal harassment. They were three in number, and well named: the Resentful, the Relentless, and the Avenger. The man dodged one, only to reel back from the lashing claws of another in one long dance of death . . .

How to defeat the Furies

These ancient deities were feared even by the Olympian gods, so it would be a tough task to neutralize the Furies. But since they pursued only those who had done wrong, people could avoid them by leading decent lives or atoning for misdeeds on Earth.

Beast Power

Strength
9

Repulsiveness
10

Special Powers
4

Ferocity
10

Invincibility
10

Total
43/50

Where does this myth come from?

In Greek mythology, the Furies had the role of punishing crimes against nature, especially murder. Even saying their name was like uttering a curse. They are mentioned by Homer in his epic poems The Iliad *and* The Odyssey, *and later, around the fifth century BCE, by Greek playwrights such as Euripides.*

Rogues' Gallery

10

The Lindwurm

In Scandinavian mythology, several lindwurms live beneath the World Tree. They try to gnaw its roots to make it topple and unbalance the universe.

9

Leyak

The hideous demon queen of the Leyak is called Rangda. She is portrayed with bulging eyes and a lolling tongue and is said to feed on children.

6

The Oni

Classic physical features of an Oni are one or several horns, an extra eye in the forehead, a gruesome grimace, and red, blue, black, or yellow skin.

5

The Seven-Headed Dragon

The Scottish seven-headed dragon was supposed to stir up a storm of wind and spray, while the East African one created a dust storm.

2

Illuyanka

In another version of the story, a goddess invites Illuyanka to a feast. He eats so much that he can no longer fit through the hole that leads back to his lair. He also becomes so sleepy that he can be tied up. Then Teshub slays him with the help of the other gods.

8

Fafnir

Fafnir was actually the son of Hreidmar the sorcerer. He turned himself into a dragon to carry off treasure that he should have shared with his family.

7

The Firedrake

The Polish firedrake not only devoured livestock but could destroy anyone with its fiery breath. It also demanded a regular meal of a fresh young maiden.

4

Echidna

Echidna's offspring were also famous monsters of Greek mythology. They included multi-headed Scylla and the dragon that guarded the Golden Fleece.

3

The Chimera

Her parents were Typhon and Echidna. Some say that the Chimera mated with the two-headed dog Orthrus to produce the Sphinx.

1

The Furies

The Furies were born from the blood of Uranus, the primeval god of the sky, who was killed by his son Kronos, a Titan god. Because they were born of a violent act, they were forever angered by any crime committed by a child against a parent. They might torment such a wrongdoer to the point of madness.

Want to Know More?

Magic Seven

For ancient peoples, seven was a magic number. The Egyptians, for example, represented evil as seven demons. Their goddess Hathor appeared in seven forms at the bedside of a newborn child. These seven Hathors were thought to predict the child's fate.

The Babylonians, who lived in the area of modern Iraq, believed in seven evil spirits that fought the gods for the souls and bodies of humans. They imagined each spirit with a different form, such as a dragon, a panther, or a hurricane. These ideas may have fused into one, to create a single dragon with seven heads. So the sevenfold ability to do harm ended up in one powerful package.

Mixing and Matching

In ancient times, the Chimera was associated with the constellation of Capricorn, which has a serpent's tail and seems to be chased away by the constellation of Pegasus in spring.

The Asiatic lion once lived around the Mediterranean: in Greece, Turkey, and the Near East. This may explain why the Chimera was part lion. So it was logical (as well as mythological!) that the Chimera gave birth to the Nemeian lion, slain by Hercules as his First Labor. The creature was also the basis of the famous dragon encountered by Saint George in medieval legend and Christian tradition.

The Chimera is perhaps the best-known mixed-up monster in the West. But other such creatures appear in legends all over the world. Some unusual combinations include the Japanese Nue, with its monkey's head, body of a raccoon dog, legs of a tiger, and serpent's tail. It could morph into a black cloud and was thought to bring misfortune.

The Aztec monster known as the Ahuizotl was half-dog, half-monkey, and its tail ended in a humanoid hand. It used this hand to drag unsuspecting humans to the depths of its watery home, where it devoured their eyes, teeth, and nails.

The word *chimera* itself has come to mean a fantastical idea, since you don't ever see such a creature in real life . . . though it's more fun to think you might!

Curse of the Ring

In the Norse myth, Fafnir's gold includes a ring, made by the dwarf Andvari, that carries a curse. As Fafnir is dying, he tells Sigurd to take his gold, but that it will harm whoever owns it. After the dragon has died, Sigurd roasts his heart and tastes the blood. This empowers him to understand the speech of birds. They warn him that Fafnir's brother Regin is planning to kill him for the treasure. Sigurd therefore also kills Regin and keeps the gold.

But indeed, all does not go well for him. Fatefully, Sigurd gives the ring to his betrothed, Brynhild, and the curse passes to her. After much plotting, shape-changing, and drinking of magic potions, Sigurd is also slain. Andvari's ring only loses its power when it sinks to the bottom of the ocean.

Norse mythology helped inspire J. R. R. Tolkien's *Lord of the Rings*. He adapted many names and ideas from ancient tales of gods, elves, dwarfs, and dragons, including the theme of the magic One Ring that passes from hand to hand and kills those who carry it.

Index

The Author

Alice Peebles is an editor and writer specializing in the arts and humanities for children. She is a coauthor of *Encyclopedia of Art for Young People* and one of the creators of *The Guzunder Gang* audiobook series. She has also edited and written for several children's magazines focused on history, art, and geography. She lives in London, England.

The Artist

Nigel Chilvers is a digital illustrator based in the United Kingdom. He has illustrated numerous children's books.

NOV 1 2 2015